I Once Knew an Indian Woman

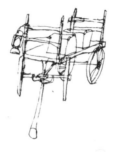

By EBBITT CUTLER

I Once Knew an Indian Woman

Illustrated by Bruce Johnson

TUNDRA BOOKS

© M. Ebbitt Cutler, 1967

Printing history

1967 First printing, Tundra Books of Montreal under the title
      THE LAST NOBLE SAVAGE, A Laurentian Idyll
      First prize, Canadian Centennial Literary Competition
1973 First US printing, Houghton-Mifflin Company, Boston,
      under the title *I ONCE KNEW AN INDIAN WOMAN*
      (This U.S. edition is now out of print. American
      customers may order directly from Tundra Books.)
      Large print edition, G.K. Hall & Company, Boston
1975 First Canadian paperback edition, Tundra Books of
      · Montreal
1976 *Reader's Digest*, Condensed Books, Canadian edition
      Sélection du Reader's Digest, Livre Condensé,
      Canadian edition
1977 *Reader's Digest*, Condensed Book, Asia edition
1978 *Reader's Digest*, Condensed Book, United Kingdom edition
1979 Second Canadian paperback edition, Tundra Books of
      Montreal
1980 French Canadian edition, *LA VIEILLE SAUVAGE*,
      translated by Maryse Côté, published by Editions Fides,
      Montreal
1985 Third Canadian paperback edition, Tundra Books

Sixth Printing

Published in Canada by   Now published in the U.S. by
Tundra Books of Montreal   Tundra Books of Northern New York
Montreal, Quebec H3G 1R4   Plattsburgh, N.Y. 12901

ISBN 0-88776-068-6

Printed in Canada

I Once Knew an Indian Woman

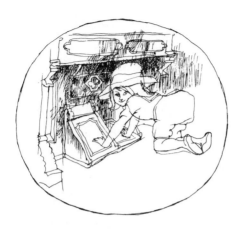

Not being the offspring of a family with any claim to distinction, not coming from a background I felt any need to live up to, or live down, I have always been impatient with those who express emotional attachment to the past. Man might not yet be perfect, but it suited me to think he was better than he had ever been. The belief that he was once wiser and kinder, more courageous and more beautiful, that he once had instinctive understanding we have lost, I dismissed as sentimental myth.

And yet I had no right to such an attitude, for I once knew a woman who was living proof of the validity of that belief. Perhaps because middle age is upon me (how painful it is to admit it like this in writing) and I recognize that more of my life now lies behind me than is likely to extend ahead, I can face other realities, which, until now, the arrogance of youth helped me ignore, and at last tell this story that has nagged at me like a suppressed but highly insistent truth all these years.

The woman I write of may well be the last noble savage to be described by an eyewitness. She does not fit into the sociological theories we use to classify our native Indians and make them manageable or, at least, excuse our inability to manage them. Not only did she survive into the twentieth century by her ancient Indian skills and values, but she shamed that world, showing up the hollowness of many of its most dearly held pretensions about itself.

Perhaps only the eyes of the child that I was could have discerned her greatness and yet, as I bring my present awareness to re-examine that old evidence, her dimensions have grown, until now, out of all the summers of my childhood, she emerges to stand in the foreground.

I was taken to the Laurentian village where she lived

for the first of my remembered summers in 1927. The lake lay less than a hundred miles north of Montreal, but it seemed very remote to me then because of the dusty four-hour train trip during which I slithered restlessly about on the varnished rattan seats while my mother gave me oranges to peel, pointed out the engine pulling us each time the train went around a turn, and warned me to "sit small" when the conductor passed to collect the tickets.

The lake was shaped like a boomerang, two miles long with the Canadian Pacific Railway tracks edging the outer rim, the railway station and village snuggling at the curve. The dirt road into the village followed the tracks as far as the station, then swerved sharply away to continue on to "the big lake" three miles farther. As I try to describe it, I see that the lake and the road really resembled *two* boomerangs placed back to back.

The village did not differ importantly from others in the Laurentians where Montrealers were already building summer cottages or vacationing in clapboard hotels, and it offered only one diversion by which one could tick off the passing of the summer days. Each evening the summer people and a few of the villagers gathered on

the platform of the railway station to watch the arrival of
the Montreal train, then moved leisurely up to the
general store a few yards away to await the sorting of

the mail. Sundays divided the weeks as fathers came from town and the tiny Roman Catholic church rang its bell at hourly intervals all morning to summon the faithful to Mass. In those first years, before the big white structure that still dominates the lake was built, the church was too small to hold everyone, and the hill behind it was crowded with hatted, high-heeled girls who climbed gingerly up the slope, helped by their coated escorts, so they could see, as well as hear, the service through the open windows.

Being of Irish Protestant parents I never attended services, but since the cottage we rented every summer for a decade was next door to the church, I was often in it. The door was always open. If I was around when the caretaker rang the bell with reasonable accuracy at seven o'clock mornings and evenings, he would let me "help" him pull the thick, rough rope. If I was around, as I had no right to be, at other times when he was not there, I would pump at a pedal of the organ in the balcony until I finally extracted a booming note that would draw my mother's attention to my absence and bring her running.

The thirty French-Canadian families that lived in the village the year round, many in unpainted, weather-grayed boxes on stilts, eked out a marginal living. They had small vegetable gardens, every inch of which had been cleared by hand from the rocky mountain slopes. A few had cows from which we got our milk "still warm." My mother, having grown up on a farm in central Ireland, was delighted by its natural state; she remarked repeatedly on its wholesomeness and flavor which she believed were spoiled in the pasteurized milk sold in the city. Also, being unseparated, it need only stand a while in the ice box to acquire a top layer of cream thick enough for whipping.

Serving the summer people was, of course, the main employment of the villagers: they worked in the hotels, did small carpentry jobs, scraped the dirt roads, cut ice from the lake for the sawdust-filled ice sheds, took in laundry, sent their daughters to work in the houses of the better-off vacationers and their children to pick and sell the wild strawberries, raspberries and blueberries that, consecutively, seemed to last the summer. Skiing had not yet opened the Laurentians to winter activity, and the men went off to the lumber camps in November to send home the fifteen dollars a month by which their families survived between summers.

Life had not always been quite so hard for them. An

industry had provided more regular employment, but it had closed down the year before our arrival. Known only as "the chemical plant," it had extracted chemicals from wood, and bits of charcoal were strewn everywhere like pebbles. For many years rumors persisted that it would re-open, but it never did, and its vast sheds and ovens became irresistible to all us children. Each afternoon terminated with the kind of ritual play that distinguishes children from adults, and makes a youngster glad he has not yet crossed the dividing line as we — yes, *we*, for even I managed occasionally to escape my mother's watchfulness on the pretext of going to the general store — flung chunks of charcoal high up the sloping tin roofs, listened as long as we dared to their bumpy trip back down, then ran to hide in the nearby woods before the only Englishman who lived year round in the village, and had, naturally, been left in charge of things by the departed English management, came out of his house the other side of the creek and shouted threateningly at us. Gradually, through the years, his interest lapsed (perhaps his stipend for looking after the property also decreased) and he went on to chicken farming while the sheds disappeared, board by board, and the tin, sheet by sheet, to repair the houses of the

7

villagers — and the children, deprived of the climax to their drama, gathered there less and less.

At the time the plant shut down, the company houses were leased out to the villagers, with the imposing hilltop residence of the former manager going to the parish priest for an unstated rental and the oldest house, a two-story unpainted box that had been vertically divided down the middle to shelter two families, going to Madame Dey for two dollars a month. Unpretentious as her house was, its location on a smaller hill just behind the station gave it a commanding view of the village and lake, and blocked the otherwise uninterrupted view from the priest's house behind it. The two properties met in a small valley between the two hills where the vegetable garden and outhouse of the one bordered on the expansive, well-kept lawn of the other.

The three of them, the priest, the Englishman and Madame Dey, formed a triangle of competing power in the village. The priest, known always as "Monsieur le curé," was a young, ascetic, bespectacled man who had, it was said, been intended for higher posts in the church but, because of a lung ailment, was assigned this little Laurentian parish where the high altitude would have a salutary effect on his health, and the small size of

the congregation a not too serious drain on his limited energy. The Englishman was known as "the king" (the English was used deliberately and never translated into "le roi"); he knew it, but the implied status of the title seemed to please him more than the sarcasm annoyed him. Madame Dey may not have known that she was referred to as "la vieille sauvage" (which the king did translate, when he spoke of her, as "the old squaw") for no one, not even the king, would have dared to call her that to her face.

In a way, I suppose, they resembled the triple forces that formed Canada itself: the religion of the French, the economic strength of the English, and the prior existence of the Indians. But while "le curé" and "the king" had establishments of considerable dimensions behind their power, Madame Dey exercised hers by personality alone — not that I wish to imply the other two were at all deficient in that sphere.

Although I could not, of course, have given so sophisticated an analysis of the three of them during my childhood, I do not think I was ever so young as not to recognize the reality of their positions.

In the end, just as it happened in Canada itself, Madame Dey was ousted from her home and forced to live on the outskirts of the village in the only vacant house she could find. The "eyesore" had to be demolished. One could not exactly blame the king; he was only carrying out orders to sell off all the company assets and Madame Dey certainly did not have the money to buy her house. Nor could one blame the curé who purchased it for the parish; it was natural that when the property came up for sale, he should be the first to want it. Heaven knows what might have been erected there, and now the view from the rectory befitted the shepherdly role of its occupant. But that was after the main events of this story, and I mention it here just to orient the reader who likes the broader politics, economics and geography clarified before he can relax and concentrate on details.

My mother was the only person I ever knew to be on friendly speaking terms with all three of them.

She was a lonely woman between my father's weekend visits. Although she was acquainted with other summer people, she felt more at home with the villagers, perhaps because their lives resembled more closely her own early farm life. She knew no French beyond a few adjectives to describe the weather like "beau" and "trempe." Few of the villagers spoke English, but she welcomed small pretexts to visit them, such as the purchase of a few stalks of rhubarb here or a head of leaf lettuce there, and she communicated in an elaborate pantomime, accompanying the gestures with unarticled English nouns. She knew all of their names, could disentangle the complex family relationships of all the Tremblays and Seguins, and — thanks to Madame Dey — knew all of the gossip concerning them.

Her friendliness to the curé was at first confined to inquiries about his health and the financial success of the annual tombola, and had a deliberateness to it. She might be Orange Irish, but "one must not be bigoted," she liked to point out to my father, who felt no similar obligation. As the curé passed our house going to and from church, she would call out to him: "And how are you feelin' today, missyew?" (Her rejection of bigotry never extended quite so far as to call him "Father," and "Monsieur le curé" seemed more French than she could manage.) He would reply in his gracious, slightly formal English with an odd little smile which I now think was occasioned by my mother's resemblance in both appearance and speech to the stereotype of the hearty Irishwoman, for often he would turn his attention immediately to me to inquire after the state of health

of the doll I always seemed to have with me. My mother was convinced that his faltering health was caused by his "having to drink all that wine Sunday mornin's without so much as a mouthful of food in his stomach," but it was some years before she presumed on her acquaintance with him sufficiently to "have a little chat" with his housekeeper and suggest he be coaxed into taking "at least a bit of an eggnog each mornin' to coat the stomach."

I thought he was quite the nicest man imaginable (perhaps because he always noticed my presence by speaking to me), and I loved the drama his tall lean figure, further elongated by his cassock, engendered as he walked by, his skirts flapping a little cloud of dust around him. He was, I realize now, the first intellectual I ever met, and both his strength and weakness as a priest perhaps derived from that. If the size of the congregation did not strain his energy, its poverty and backwardness did — so much so that he was to become a model priest in the Laurentians. More than any other individual he was responsible for developing the area as one of Canada's greatest ski resorts, personally spearheading negotiations between government and private enterprise, so that his people might have work the year round. He not only had the new church built, but, as soon as he could, arranged for the building of a good-sized, well-equipped schoolhouse. During the depression years when one of the large hotels remained closed, he put it into service as a youth hostel. To find vegetables more suitable to the soil and climate of the village, he built a greenhouse where he experimented with seeds and seedlings which he provided to the farmers. The last time I remember hearing his voice was on an English-language news broadcast during the forties when a snow drought kept the ski hills brown until March and the hotels empty. He was asking Montrealers to send food for his unemployed parishioners.

But like many intellectuals, even practical intellectuals, he was not at his best in the moments of great private tragedy that strike nearly all families at one time or another. The display of uncontrolled emotion seemed to embarrass him. As required by his calling, he attended the deathbeds and officiated at the funerals, but he limited such contacts to the minimum, and his parishioners, much as they appreciated his efforts on their behalf, never quite felt he was one of them.

The king, on the other hand, never was and never wanted to be identified in any way with the villagers.

He was English-English, as distinguished from Canadian-English. I have long forgotten what part of England he came from but some of his idioms fascinated me: he always "knowed" or "knewed" everything. A ruddy-faced man with a reddish-gray barbershop-quartet mustache, he walked with his thumbs inserted under his suspenders; these were stretched to their limit over a Humpty-Dumpty stomach and held his trouser legs well above the ankle. He cowed his wife, a tiny, tight-lipped woman who crocheted lace tablecloths and doilies with compulsive ferocity, never spoke a word in his presence, and never stopped talking outside of it. Her occasional visits to our cottage were not welcomed with much enthusiasm by my mother, who claimed, "I can never get a word in edgewise with that woman." Not that my mother got many words in "edgewise," or otherwise, with the king, but I think she was flattered that he seemed to like to talk to her.

Besides being rent collector and caretaker for the departed chemical company, he looked after "things" for those summer people who rented out their cottages when they were not using them. That is not to imply he *repaired* anything; merely that he received complaints which he transmitted to the owners. The cottage we

rented was one of these. My mother's first visits to his house, which lay at the other end of the village beyond the station and general store, were instigated by a leak in the woodshed roof and the running dry of the well; we saw him more frequently after she decided to buy her weekend chickens from him because "at least he kills them dead." During our first summers she had bought them from the farmer who delivered our milk, but this terminated one Saturday morning when she opened the newspaper-wrapped parcel and found the chicken to be still alive — not what one would call lively, but alive, nonetheless. She had, as she told my father later, "the very devil of a time killing it," and even after she beheaded it outside on the grass with an axe, its legs waved at her reproachfully. She was far from being squeamish, but a chicken that would not die posed metaphysical problems which a woman in a hurry to get a bird plucked, cleaned out, stuffed and into the oven has neither the time nor the desire to ponder.

The king refused to take advance orders and deliver his chickens; he was known as a penny pincher, and the neighboring children kept out of his way, for they did not seem to feel that the *noblesse oblige* he displayed in asking them to run messages made up for the lack of more tangible remuneration. On Friday afternoons when we appeared, he would lead us grandly up to his pullet houses, ask my mother which particular bird she fancied, and with impressive efficacy catch it, string it up by the legs, and kill it on the spot with a special hooked knife. I was never quite certain that it was the exact chicken she had selected from the gray-feathered clucking flock, but *he* was certain, and my mother never challenged his choice. He had, I realize now, something that can silence superfluous quibbling among adults and absolutely overawe children: style.

I would watch these killings, waiting for the moment of stillness with shivery, but unquestioning, fascination. It was not until some years later, when I recounted to a city school friend how I had seen many chickens killed and was looked at with horror, that I felt I must have been deficient in some basic decency to have stood by and willingly witnessed such bloody scenes.

The king, carrying the dead chicken like a trophy, would then lead us down the hill to his house. The living room impressed me with its elaborate furnishings, in contrast to the utilitarian modesty of the summer cottages and the austerity of the villagers' houses, where all living, other than sleeping, went on in the kitchen. He would order his wife to wrap the chicken, seat himself in a gigantic, black, leather-covered easy chair beside a lace-covered table, motion my mother to a straight-backed dining room chair, pick up one of the farm papers he subscribed to and bring us up to date on the state of chicken farming. I don't think my mother, in spite of her farm background, understood these reports on feed mixtures, breeds and egg wholesaling any more than I did, but she made appropriate interjections and, as soon as she could do so politely, turned the conversation to what both she and I never tired of hearing: his stories of the Great War. Meanwhile, the chicken duly wrapped, his wife would take her place on another dining room chair next to the piano that was never played and silently crochet, rather, I realize now, like a suspicious and disapproving chaperon.

He had been a sergeant during the war — was ever man more suited to the job? — and his stories of life in the trenches of France made that muddy miserable world more real to me than all the accounts, photographs and films I have seen since. He had been wounded by shrapnel on his left side, and his hand often moved there to massage it gently as he talked. Neither the ribbons and medals framed above the piano, nor the numerous photographs of him in breeches hanging on the other walls, dramatized his involvement as did that movement of his hand. "I'm just a hollow shell inside," he once said proudly. "They cut out everything. The last time the doctor came at me with the knife, he said: 'That's it, soldier. It's no use coming back here.'" His stomach became for me a mystery to contemplate, like a vast, empty cave; I was eye level with it for much of this story, and when he stood up, his suspenders stretched up the long slope to his head like tracks over a mountain.

In some ways he fancied himself the English gentleman: his war pension made him independent; his rent collecting was certainly appropriate to the pretension; and his chicken farming was carried on with the scientific, but enthusiastic, precision of the English amateur who can pursue a hobby the more ardently, the less he depends on it for a livelihood. That is how I see him now. As I stood beside my mother or sat on the hassock he would nudge towards me with his foot. As a child I saw him as Old Kaspar in Southey's poem of the Battle of Blenheim and myself as little Wilhelmine looking up "with wonder-waiting eyes" and asking: "Now tell us about the war,/And what they fought each other for." I knew many lines of it, for my father, a quiet, watery-eyed southern Irishman whom my mother seemed forever to be waking from a dream, would often recite it aloud to himself. He was tone-deaf and declaimed poetry as others sing songs; his preference, with the exception of the Psalms, was for verse with a strong story line and a military setting. High among his favorites were Mrs. Hemans' "Casabianca" ("The boy stood on the burning deck/Whence all but he had fled") and Charles Wolfe's "Burial of Sir John Moore" ("Slowly and sadly we laid him down,/From the field of his fame fresh and gory;/We carved not a line, and we raised not a stone —/But we left him alone with his glory"). Oddly English for an Irishman? My father's ancestors had come to Ireland with Cromwell, and he had come to Canada, he said, "Because I wanted to die as I was born, under the Union Jack." His wish came true by a narrow margin: he died the year before Canada adopted its own flag. But I must not spend time talking about him here, for he plays little role in this summer story. Unlike my mother, he was not sociable, and on weekends after meals (during which he was a captive audience for her reports on the week's events) he would sit in the sun in the garden to doze and perhaps to dream of those old heroics on which his youth was fed. I found it odd then, though I no longer do, that he took little interest in the king's realistic accounts of an actual battle-field: the romance of wars increases, the greater one's distance from them.

Like the children sitting at Old Kaspar's feet, I never did find out what that war was all about, and to this day I am not too sure I know. However, in those days when we had neither television nor radio and very few books, the stories told by the king were very important to me. He was the best storyteller I knew, with one exception.

That exception was Madame Dey, and it was her house we visited almost daily through a decade of summers.

My mother's meeting with her was auspicious. I don't know if I was really present on the occasion, or if I just *think* I was because my mother described it so often to so many people. (She seemed to feel she had to justify her friendship with Madame Dey.) It was our first summer there and I developed a feverish cold which my mother believed would only respond if my chest were treated to a rub of camphorated oil. She was asking for it in the general store without success when a deep booming voice came at her from behind in English: "Pardon me, madam, but I know where you can get camphorated oil." My mother turned and there stood Madame Dey: a giant of a woman in a Mother Hubbard skirt with men's socks and shoes (her huge feet could be contained in nothing less), short straight black hair clipped tightly to the side of her head with a bobby pin, great black half-moon eyes reaching out over high cheekbones and a single large front tooth emphasizing the absence of its companion. My mother, not one to be put off by physical appearances as long as a friendly voice accompanied them, confessed that on this occasion, she was "quite taken aback. T'was as if she'd come out of the airth."

Madame Dey not only told her where she could get the medicine but walked her a mile and a half south from the village to the farmer who ran a bootleg drugstore from a room off his kitchen. He had an impressive assortment of remedies, both home and patented, from which he even prescribed when requested.

The friendship that developed between the two women was based on more than gratitude on my mother's side: she had discovered the only woman villager who could speak English. Madame Dey actually spoke more correct English than she spoke French, for she had learned it working as a servant in upper-middle-class English homes, whereas her French, learned first from her husband and not much enriched by the French-Canadian laborers and farmers among whom she lived, remained on the *patois* level or, as it is now called, *joual*. Her first language was Iroquois.

Since Madame Dey's house was the oldest building in the village, its strategic location was understandable enough. So was its appearance. Its unpainted wood had mellowed during the thirty or forty years it had been washed by rain and snow, until its deep gray appeared black from the distance and the black was further emphasized by the white-painted trim on the door and window frames where rot tends to attack. Its two stories had been divided down the center between two front doors leading into the respective dwelling units. It was possible to go from one to the other without going outside, for a doorway had been broken through between the two all-purpose kitchens that took up the ground floor, but Madame Dey kept it closed all day in summer. She made her living by doing laundry for the summer people who had "homes" (as distinct from the "cottages" in our village) at the big lake up the road. In the right-hand kitchen her vast wood stove burned all day long to keep the oval tubs of sheets boiling and her collection of irons warm. The ironing itself she did in the cooler left-hand kitchen, carrying the irons back and forth by the *outside* entrances. This detour into the open air not only served to cool her off, but provided a view of everything going on around the general store and station, and on nearly the whole expanse of the lake itself. Her shout of greeting or inquiry to any villager who passed on foot or wagon was one of the most familiar sounds in the area, welcome to some, like my mother, and embarrassing to others.

The king particularly resented her inclusion of him in this indiscriminate camaraderie. He referred to her contemptuously as "Mrs. In-One-Door-and-Out-the-Other," and I suspect that the detours he often made across the creek and through the chemical company grounds to get from one side of the village to the other were motivated more by a desire to avoid her shouts than the need to keep an eye on his obligations. For though she always shouted to him in English, her questions of "How are the chickens today?" or "Is there going to be another war?" reduced him to the level of the villagers, a declassing he hated and which she, with her infallible

instinct for recognizing pretentiousness, pursued with amusement. She believed he would, if he could, have her evicted from her perch, but in those early years she was confident that the promise of protection given her by the departed company manager's wife would keep her safe. Nonetheless she was always careful to get her rent in on time, telling her foster daughter who was sent with the two dollars not to surrender it unless the king was home and gave a receipt.

My mother and I would never go to the general store without dropping in (or up) to see Madame Dey. Evenings, my mother would often wait there while I went to the post office to get the mail, then stay on reading tidbits from the *Montreal Star* by the light of an oil lamp which Madame Dey removed from its nail on the wall and placed on a table for the purpose. Madame Dey would sit listening avidly, her big hands moving incessantly over her knitting, to my mother's very personal selection of crime news from page three (to which my mother added editorial comment by way of sighs, tut-tutting and rhetorical questions about what the world was coming to). Only when my mother would glance in shocked surprise at the clock, declare determinedly, "The child must be got to bed," and start to fold the

paper would Madame Dey interrupt to inquire plead-
ingly: "Do they say anything about California in there,
madam?" My mother would shake her head and promise
to search the paper more carefully the following day.
Even when she found California datelines, she refused
to report them to Madame Dey, who, she believed, was
already worried enough about her youngest son without hearing of "the goings on of those wild actresses."

Gene, according to his mother, was the handsomest
and cleverest of her four sons, and since her other sons,
all of whom were married and lived in the village, were
certainly good-looking, he must have been quite strik-
ing. We never met him, but we did see him once in
the distance, running down the path from her house to
a convertible where a blond woman sat waiting. He
was wearing plus fours which, in those days, we asso-
ciated with the Prince of Wales and the international
set. In the village we saw the rich, distant, dis-
solute world as only a cloud of dust left by the big
open touring cars and roadsters that sped back and forth
from the expensive, elegant hotels at the big lake. Gene
had been working as a bellhop at the hotel that stood
on a cliff overlooking the big lake when he met the
woman. Whether she was widowed or divorced, I was

never told, but she was fifteen years older than Gene, and when she invited him to go back to California with her as her "chauffeur," he accepted. I could not understand in those days why Madame Dey was so upset over the arrangement; it seemed to me she ought to have been proud that Gene had been given such an opportunity to advance himself. But Madame Dey, I now realize, understood precisely the implications of the arrangement and while she might be helpless to stop it, she

would not be cajoled into pretending to approve. For the first few years after he left, letters came from Gene's "employer" every few months, then they dropped to one a year and, finally, stopped altogether. Madame Dey would always carry the last one received in her bosom, and would ask my mother to read it over to her from time to time, as if she hoped to understand more in each reading. There was certainly little information in them ("Gene is fine and sends his love. Perhaps we will get east this summer, and he will be able to visit you"). They were written in what my mother called "a fine hand" on tinted stationery, with the woman's name and address engraved on both the note paper and the lined envelopes. Gene himself never wrote. He had gone to the village school longer than her other children, but the six grades taught in one room (where most of the teacher's energy, it was said, went to keep discipline) never seemed to have prepared anyone to do more than write his name and recite his catechism.

At least once each summer, my mother would bring her own pad and pen over to Madame Dey's to write a reply on her behalf. Each letter ended with the same words: "Mrs. Dey wants you to send Gene home."

Because of the laundry, Madame Dey's house — both

sides of it — always smelled of Javelle water and starch. Behind it, strung across her vegetable garden, long lines of sheets and shirts waved snappingly. The thin French-Canadian from the city who ran the post office–general store as if it were a short-staffed military headquarters under perpetual siege had little time for pleasantries. (The stacks of bill books of accounts owing him, filed alphabetically behind the counter, could not have reassured him much that the siege would ever let up.) But he seemed to start each day optimistically, and for those customers who appeared before 11 A.M. he even managed a smile and a reference to the weather; he said he could always tell whether an uncertain morning would clear or not simply by looking out to see if Madame Dey had put up her wash.

Sharing the house with her were Madame Dey's married daughter whose husband worked as a handyman for a hotel at the big lake, her daughter's baby — soon to be added to annually — and a little girl of my age with long black pigtails and a pretty name: Amande? Yolande? Fernande? (How odd that I should have forgotten exactly, when it was such a nice word to say.) Amande, as I shall call her, never knew her real mother and father. She had been taken in when a few days old

33

by Madame Dey, an act of charity my mother often referred to when she defended Madame Dey against charges of her being "a character." "She's a good heart, that woman," my mother would say. "It's not many as would take somebody else's baby into the house, after bringing up six of her own, and her not getting a red cent for it either."

Amande was a very quiet child whom I cannot remember ever laughing. I found this quite understandable. Would not a tragedy so impenetrable as to lose one's parents when one was too young to know what was happening not condition anyone forever to sadness? In those early years my French learned on our east-end Montreal street was restricted to words for toys, food and clothing, and to expressions essential for play such as "tiens," "ma va" and "vas t'en." I could not, therefore, question her about it, and my mother warded off my persistent inquiries as to how precisely a catastrophe of such magnitude could come about with "Ye're too young to understand such things" until, finally, when I was no longer too young to understand, I no longer needed to ask.

Although I could sit as happily as my mother and listen to Madame Dey's stories of the human experience based on her own life and that of others (she was already well over fifty when we met her), I was often sent out to play with Amande while they had "grown-up" talk. Our "play" always took the form of helping out. We would bring in the split logs for Madame Dey's stove, search for carrots large enough to pull in the vegetable garden and, best of all, pick bugs off the potato plants. For this chore, Amande put a few inches of water from the garden pump into two of the tall green bleach bottles so that once the bugs were dropped in, they could not climb back out. Together we worked methodically up and down the rows of potato plants, stopping from time to time to match bottles and see who had the larger collection. Finding the lively hard-backed orange bugs, which I could not distinguish from lady bugs, and watching them drop down inside the green glass held a magic for me that no berry-picking, which it somewhat resembled, could ever match.

Madame Dey's other children, with the exception, of course, of her beloved Gene in California, had children of their own and lived much as the other villagers. Only one of them, Leo, carried on his Indian heritage. He was a toweringly slim man who walked with sprintlike strides, raising and putting down his feet as if testing the

firmness of the ground. He worked as a guide, and had the reputation of never coming back empty-handed from a fishing or hunting trip, even though most of the lakes in the area were said to be "fished out," and the partridges were already scared away by the time the trees were sufficiently bare of leaves for amateurs to sight them. The uncertainty of his income (further aggravated by his drinking) and the poverty of his family were a continual cause of worry to Madame Dey, who immediately sent the used clothing my mother gave her at the end of each summer to Leo's long-suffering wife. But in spite of his dislike of regular work, he still managed to build his family a house with wood and corrugated tin filched from the abandoned chemical plant. I don't know who owned the land on the frog pond, as we called it, halfway between our lake and the big lake, where he put the structure, for no one protested his right to it, but the stolen materials were another matter. By the time the king learned of this brash concentrated displacement of company property, the house was as finished as it would ever be. He visited Leo in an imperious rage and ordered its return, but he was neither prepared to accept the hammer Leo offered him, by way of answer, and dismantle it himself, nor willing to pay anyone else to do it. And Leo only laughed off his threats to call the provincial police, for he knew that not even the king would dare to intrude such an outside force into the self-regulating life of the village. There was a provincial police office in a town ten miles away, but I know of no occasion, not even during the emergency that is the main incident of this account, when it was ever called for help.

"Besides," as the king told my mother, rationalizing his impotence, "I never seed such a shack. Even the walls were covered with tin. They won't be able to live out the winter in it." Then he sniffed, his gray-red mustache moving with the contemptuous curve of his lips: "He'll go the way of his father yet. I always say if the father's no good, what can you expect of the son?"

They did, however, not only manage to pass their first winter in it but many another, and were still living there the last summer I spent at the lake. As for the reference to Leo's father, it was true the son seemed to have inherited, or acquired, his father's intemperance, but the king's syllogism was scarcely valid since Madame Dey's other sons in the village were sober enough.

The only time I ever saw tears in Madame Dey's great black eyes was when she spoke of her late husband.

He had died the winter before our first summer at the lake and she seemed to miss him very much, although, in my mother's view, "she was well rid of him." From the moment at the age of fifteen when she left her father's house on the Indian reservation of Caughnawaga to "run away" with Georges Dey, until the January morning when he was found dead in the snow, she never questioned his right to her roof and bed. He had walked out on her countless times during their marriage, leaving her to feed and shelter their children without help, and returning sometimes after as long as a year's absence without money to show for it. "But why would you take him back?" my mother would say. I remember Madame Dey once answering: "Can the hunter help it if he must sometimes return with empty hands?"

My mother, of course, regarded Georges Dey's death in the snow as God's justice. She, too, could quote verse, usually sayings culled from sermons she had heard. The one she repeated most often as a kind of epitaph to the late Mr. Dey was: "The mills of God grind slowly, yet they grind exceeding small;/Though with patience He stands waiting, with exactness grinds He all."

It was usually in our house and not hers that

Madame Dey talked of her husband. Perhaps lone-liness brought her over for that express purpose. She would visit us a few evenings each summer (though never, of course, on weekends) if my mother had not been in to see her for a day or two. Her loud shout of "Are you in?" announced her coming long before she reached the steps of our cottage, much to my mother's mortification. In the stillness that falls over Laurentian lakes at twilight, my mother was sure the shout could be heard clear across to the far shore. Sometimes she would bring a photograph from a newspaper that had wrapped laundry to ask my mother to read the caption. Always she would have in the large hidden pockets of her mountainous skirt some knitting to work on while she talked, as if having something in her hands disci-plined her emotions.

She met Georges Dey one summer when he was work-ing with a repair gang on the road that ran through the reservation. She had never been farther than a few miles from it in her life, not even across the river to Montreal; nor had she ever attended the reservation school where boys were given a rudimentary knowledge of the languages they would need to find work outside the reservation. The confinement of the girls was in-

41

tentional, for the tribe believed that as long as the girls remained at home, the boys would return. Women must give the society its continuity, must wait until the young men passed the age of impetuousness, remembered their history, assumed their obligations to the tribe and acquired the proud defiance that was its only protection against the encroachments of the invaders. When her father told stories of the Iroquois past, so immediate were the descriptions that she assumed the invaders had come only a few years before his birth.

She was also given to believe, though she could not remember being told it in words, that if the tribe remained true to its birthright, it would own everything back again some day, even the great evil city across the water.

She could not remember a time when she did not know how to sew and knit and clean and cook. (Perhaps Amande's seriousness was like her own as a child.) At the age of eleven she had assisted in the delivery of a baby sister, her mother calling out the directions between spasms as matter-of-factly as if ordering the preparation of a meal.

On Saturday nights when the young men returned to the reservation, bringing illegal liquor with them, the girls were kept in the house and could hear the shouts and singing and fighting of the men around the long house. The first non-Indians she ever saw were the police who raided the reservation. When they entered the house searching for liquor, her mother sat with stony immobility waiting for the desecration to stop, then she would get up and without a word replace each object in its appointed place. Where drawers had been opened, every piece of clothing was removed, shaken out and refolded. "She wanted it as if they'd never been in the house," Madame Dey said. Since all men in the city were in her mind either drunkards or policemen, it did not seem impossible that the whole reservation might rise up some night after the city had drunk itself into a stupor, kill the policemen, and capture it.

But Georges Dey was not at all like the sinister intruders. He laughed all the time. The first day he saw her on the road, he teasingly coaxed her toward him, holding out a sandwich from his lunch bag. "I took it and ran off like a squirrel," she recalled, "and like a squirrel I went back the next day." He talked all the time in French. The first French word she learned was "viens" as he held out the food to her; soon he offered chocolate, and if she held back he would eat a piece himself to show her it was good and then proffer the rest. After two weeks, when the road work was finished and he said "Viens," she went with him. "I knew they would never come after me, and I knew I could never go back — I was a bird fallen from the nest."

He took her to the city to live with a sister who arranged for them to be married, and the next few months were the happiest of her life. When he left to go on another job, she was pregnant. Thus the pattern of her married life was established. She accepted his drinking at first as a matter of course. Did not all men drink? And even after she learned that this was not so, her Indian loyalty sustained her. In the first years he always returned bringing presents and money; then, as he discovered that she could support herself and the children without him, he returned with only apologies, like a naughty child to its mother. She worked as a day servant, leaving her children at first to the care of his sister and later with anyone who would look after them. When she moved the family, she always made sure to leave word where he might find her.

They moved to the Laurentians when Georges, during one of his resolutions to reform, took a job with the chemical company. For the ten years before his death,

44

he was in and out of work with the company, which, though it fired him frequently for drunkenness, rehired him whenever it was short-staffed. "Everyone liked him," Madame Dey said. "He was a good worker when he worked. He was happy all the time, like Leo. The company manager once told me that the others worked better when he was around, that he coaxed them into getting things done. If only they could have been sure when he left Saturdays that he'd be back sober on Mondays, he might have been their top foreman."

Perhaps it was the closing down of the company that ended hope for him, for where else could he, a man in his sixties, find so sympathetic an employer? Shortly before his death he had started to steal things from the house to buy beer, little ornaments he had given her as presents through the years. It also seemed that the less money he had for drink, the lower went his tolerance level. The night before the one on which he died, he had gone out and come back around eleven o'clock, woken up their daughter, and demanded money from her husband's pay which had arrived that day from the lumber camp. Madame Dey was awakened by her daughter's screams to find her husband holding the baby above his head and threatening to knock its brains out if he were not given the money.

"Something happened inside me when I saw that," Madame Dey recalled, and I can still see her the one and only time she recounted that particular part of the story in detail; her hands tight around her knitting, her half-moon eyes staring beyond us into the wall as if she saw it being re-enacted on a screen there. "Grandchildren are different to your own. They don't belong to you. They're a gift you have given the world to show you think it is good and should go on after you. I would have killed him if he'd hurt that child. I don't remember what I said, but he put the baby down and went to bed . . . and I decided I would never allow him into the house drunk again."

It was the following night that, returning to find the doors bolted against him and lacking either the energy or heart to make it to the barn of one of his drinking friends, he lay down to sleep in the snow.

Often in talking about her husband, Madame Dey would put down her knitting, take a piece of neatly cut sheeting from her bosom, wipe her eyes and blow her nose, while my mother searched among her collection of religious quotations to find one to sum it all up. If God's

mills were not grinding slowly, then He was working "in a mysterious way His wonders to perform" and there was to "everything a season and a time to every purpose under heaven."

The protectiveness of the company manager's wife towards Madame Dey, and her promise that "as long as the company owned the house, she would have a roof over her head," arose from Madame Dey's experience in midwifery. The manager's wife, as was the fashion of the time, took a patronizing interest in the illnesses of the village families, particularly in the arrival of new children. It upset her that they should be born with just any convenient neighbor in attendance, and when she discovered Madame Dey's experience in making deliveries, she set her up as the village midwife. A pattern was established: when the wife of an employee went into labor, word was sent to the manager's wife, who, in turn, sent word to Madame Dey (who lived so conveniently close by). Madame Dey would gather together the bundle of clean sheets and blankets she kept ready for the purpose and answer the call. Afterwards Madame Dey would receive a fee of fifty cents for her work. It was a kind of company insurance plan covering births which the manager's wife set up voluntarily; her reward was to visit the new arrival later and receive the flattering gratitude of the family. Since she realized that the success of her whole scheme depended on Madame Dey's skill, she naturally had, as my mother liked to phrase it; "a soft spot in her heart for you." And Madame Dey's proprietory interest in the affairs of all the villagers was equally understandable. Many of her shouts to the farmers who passed her house referred to their continuing fertility.

With the closing of the plant and the ending of the delivery scheme, the village women reverted to their former cooperative system and Madame Dey was less frequently called. Few babies seemed to arrive in summer. Indeed, I can remember only one, an eighth child born to Madame Dey's other daughter, who had married an Italian immigrant and lived near the big lake. When we visited the mother in the late afternoon to see the baby that had been born early that morning, she was already up and making supper for her family.

Much as I loved to hear Madame Dey tell about her early life and the village as it was before we arrived, what I liked most about her was something else, something I can only sum up with the word "elegance."

A strange word to apply to one so huge of body, and so heavy of foot?

It was the way she did things, the care she took. She ironed cotton sheets as if they were made of silk and men's shirts as if they belonged to a lover. Remembering those neat rows of baskets along her wall with the clothes flawlessly folded and waiting to be picked up, and thinking of the machine-washed and machine-ironed clothes our laundries send back today with, as my mother would have said, "all the good taken out of them," I wonder if those women with summer "homes" at the big lake appreciated her. Perhaps they did, for Madame Dey bragged that she never lost a customer. Even her house, in spite of the sparse furnishings, seemed arranged with conscious care; the rough wooden floors were almost white for, again to use my mother's words, "they were scrubbed to the bone." Her vegetable garden was planted so neatly one would think the distance between each seed had been measured with a ruler. Amande's white pinafores were starched like those of children in picture books; her own vast skirts, which she made from flour bags and dyed black, fell in folds as neat as a nun's. When she combed and braided Amande's hair and snapped on an elastic band to hold the ends, not a single strand hung loose. Only in the braided upswept hair of ballet dancers have I since seen such perfection.

It was strange to watch hands so large, larger even than my father's, with square tips and tight-cropped nails, perform delicate tasks like threading a needle. Even that she did as if she were challenged to get the thread through the hole on the first try. Did she believe that the magic she performed in small household matters would somehow stretch beyond them to create orderliness in the life of her family?

Each summer, usually around the second or third week in August, her front doors would remain closed until evening and we would know, for she usually forewarned us, that she was away picking blueberries. She would start out around six in the morning, carrying the big empty lard pails, a lunch for herself and Amande, and walk the three miles to the big lake and another mile

into the woods where she knew the blueberries grew in quantity. Sometimes we were waiting for her when she arrived home in the late afternoon, for she would have suggested that we stop in to get some from her. She would walk up the hill to her house, her step heavy under the weight of the pails (my mother marveled that she could lift them at all, let alone carry them so far), Amande following her, carrying two smallish pails that were used for the actual picking. Her face would light up when she saw us. Inside she would take off her men's shoes, remove her woolen socks and put her feet into a basin of water, talking all the time triumphantly of her day. "Look at them," she would say, pointing to the pails, "not a green berry, not a leaf." Her feet washed and dried, she would get up and pour the huge pails slowly into assorted smaller bowls and pails, again pointing out the cleanness of her pickings as they fell, a waterfall of rolling blue marbles. I have always loved to tip a box of blueberries into a sieve for washing since then and, picking out the unripe berry, the overripe berry, a leaf or a twiggy stem, remember.

She had brought her children up in her husband's religion, but, except for a reproduction of the Sacred Heart on her wall (perhaps put there by one of her children), she never showed any interest in it and never attended services in the church. She ignored the curé with noticeable contempt for his youth and his avoidance of crises. "What does he understand?" she once said to my mother, and my mother found herself in the ironical position of defending him (a role I think she was pleased to assume) with the reply: "They say he's got a good head on his shoulders."

Caughnawaga in her youth had a Catholic mission on it, but I got the impression from her that the Christianity practiced was far from purist. I remember her once saying: "When you have many gods, at least you can choose among them," an interesting rejection of the tyranny of monotheism, it seems to me now, which perhaps formed the basis of her skepticism. My mother, never short of platitudes, would reassure her, with only slight condescension: "You can be good if ye never went to church."

But, it seemed to me, Madame Dey's memory and intelligence showed up most remarkably in, of all things, her knitting. It was a time when women wore sweaters knitted in elaborate lacy patterns of fans, flowers and leaves done, not with different color yarn, but by intricate increasing, decreasing, slipping and passing over of stitches. Every such sweater Madame Dey saw challenged her, and usually she could analyze a design simply by looking at it. Her laundry customers often gave her their old sweaters, and one night I remember her ripping out such a sweater, so matted that it looked undecipherable, and *memorizing the stitch backwards*. My mother, who had trouble following a pattern described in a magazine or newspaper, was astonished at the feat and talked about it as we walked home that night with the beam from our flashlight bouncing ahead of us. "There's not a thing that woman can't do," she said, "except read and write."

I have often wondered if the reason she remained illiterate was not by deliberate choice — as if the role assigned to women by her tribe exercised a continuing inhibition, as if she had betrayed them enough by leaving them and wished to witness to their inherent capacity by living within their limitations, as if she wanted to show that an Indian could survive in a white man's world without a white man's weapons. Just as she had brought her Indian loyalty to an undeserving white husband and could endure with dignity conditions that would have defeated most other women, so she seemed to bring a faith that the ancient attributes and talents of her race would see her through. Perhaps her rejection of Christianity had a similar basis.

She was doomed, of course, doomed to be undervalued, ridiculed and discounted — I write this in the hope that she will not be forgotten — just as her house was doomed to be demolished, just as her race seemed doomed to be absorbed. Her grandchildren were already indistinguishable from the other children of the village. Yet she had her moment of glory. When the crisis occurred and the whole social structure of the village seemed paralyzed, she emerged with primitive magnificence to suggest that courage and kindness perhaps once existed to a greater degree in our land than we have ever imagined.

I was thirteen that summer and had stopped accompanying my mother to visit Madame Dey. Conformity to social pressures was becoming important, and I was aware that she was regarded as an oddball, an eccentric, a character. One evening in early August when she came to visit us, I remained upstairs in my room reading.

"You hurt Madame Dey by not coming down to speak to her," my mother said afterwards. "She asked me if perhaps you didn't like her coming here anymore."

"She's right," I said sullenly, "none of the other summer people have her to their houses. Why do we have to?"

"You're getting to be the snotty one, aren't you?" my mother retorted. "I'll have ye know that as long as I live she's welcome here, and you'll be civil, or I'll have it out with your father."

The argument turned out to be unnecessary, I am sorry to write, for although after the tragedy I went back to visiting her and she always greeted me as warmly as ever, she never came to visit us at home again.

It wasn't much of a tragedy really, so small and inconsequential that it took only four lines in the *Montreal Star* two days later, but it was my first contact with accidental death, and, because of Madame Dey, the most dramatic event I have ever experienced.

Who brought us the first news of it, I don't remember. Perhaps a passing farmer. It was late August and, although the nights came early and were chilly with a touch of fall, the day had been warm and beautiful. I was changing after my swim when my mother rushed in, shouting: "There's been a drowning in the lake!"

Outside, as we stood scanning the water, we could see a large number of rowboats at a far point along the railway track.

"They're bringing the body back now," my mother said. "It's somebody staying at the hotel near the station." At the main wharf a crowd had gathered, awaiting the arrival of the rowboats. As more people passed on the road, they stopped to give details.

No one knew the drowned man. He had arrived by train only that noon, told the hotel he wanted a swim before lunch and had taken out a rowboat. When he did not return, the hotel keeper sent out his son, who found the boat up at the point, empty except for a towel, wallet and wrist watch.

The lake was typically Laurentian in that one could usually judge the slope beneath the water by the slope of the mountainside at the edge. The drowning occurred at a little sandy strip which belonged to the railway and was considered "public." People went to it by boat or by walking up the track. Although it was a popular place to swim, it was also considered dangerous, for here the sandy bottom stretched out to a depth of four or five feet, then dropped sharply exactly where a person wading would not be able to see the bottom and would assume the gradualness to continue.

"We'll have our supper, then we'll go to see Madame Dey," my mother said. "She'll know all about it."

When we arrived at Madame Dey's, her daughter told us in French that she was at the station. There was a crowd on the platform and we went down to

58

find Madame Dey arguing with the station master. She stopped to explain to us: the hotel had refused to take the body in; the dead man's parents had been telephoned in the city and they were coming up by the evening train, which that year did not come in until nine-thirty (the schedule changed annually between seven and ten for reasons the Canadian Pacific Railway alone knew).

"They can't just leave him there like that," Madame Dey complained, "for his parents to come and find him."

A few feet away the crowd parted and we saw what she meant. The body lay, naked except for swimming trunks, on the wagon used to transport suitcases. My mother gasped. It was the first time I had seen a dead person outside a coffin; the death pangs were still evident in the staring eyes and distorted mouth, and the horror seemed magnified by the brutal way the iron of the wagon pressed against his flesh.

Like a crowd at an accident, feeling helpless and uncertain, the people questioned each other: Why was he there? Why wouldn't the hotel take him in? Had the curé been told? Couldn't the curé speak to the hotel keeper? Someone had been to tell the curé, it seemed, but the curé never appeared.

My mother saw the king among the crowd and we went over to him. He stood apart, surveying the scene, his thumbs under his suspenders, the white cotton business shirt he always wore, tieless and with the sleeves rolled up, emphasizing his separateness.

"The hotel won't take the body in," my mother said.

"His relatives can sue them for that," the king commented, his mustache twitching.

"Maybe if ye were to go to the hotel and tell them that . . ." my mother said tentatively.

The king shrugged: "It's no affair of mine," then added: "I don't see why they're all in such a hurry to be going into the lake. I've lived here well on twenty years and I never knowed the need. I wash at home."

We went back to where Madame Dey was standing beside the station master and my mother reported the king's comment about the hotel being liable. The station master, a mild man who had been transferred to the village only that year, looked uncomfortable. Why should he be burdened with something no one else wanted? It couldn't be there on the platform when the train arrived. Finally, in desperation, he picked up the handles of the wagon, pushed it into the baggage room, slid the door to, locked it and told everyone to go away.

We walked with Madame Dey slowly back up the hill to her house. "We can't leave the boy like that for his parents to find," she said, over and over. As we reached the door of her house, she stopped suddenly. "I'm going to bring him here," she announced.

"Your'e *not!*" my mother said, aghast. "You're not going to bring a dead body into your house!"

"I am," she said, and we followed her back to the station, hypnotized by her plan.

"Take it if you want it." The station master shrugged. He unlocked the baggage room door and went back to his office. Madame Dey looked at the dead man, put out her hand and forced his eyes closed; then lifting the handles of the wagon, she pushed it outside.

On the platform the station master reappeared. The wagon belonged to the railway company. He could not allow it off railway property. Madame Dey looked at him as if she wanted to memorize his face, then she bent over and raised the body onto her shoulders.

"You can't!" my mother protested, close to hysteria. "It's too heavy."

"Go home, go home, madam. I'm all right," she said, and we watched, transfixed.

She moved slowly, staggering a little under the weight, a huge black figure with the head and arms of the dead man flopping terribly down her back. The crowd regathered; cars passing on the road stopped; but no one moved to help her. When at last she reached her front door, a sigh of relief seemed to go up.

I remember that we walked home in silence. For once my mother did not attempt to sum things up. I went to my room and lay on the bed, staring at the boards in the ceiling until darkness fell, then I turned and gazed out the window at the lights flickering on across the lake. I did not hear my mother come in until she spoke: "I want to go back. Will you come with me?"

Only the left-hand door of Madame Dey's house stood open as we walked up the path. Inside, the room where she did her ironing had been transformed. A white sheet covered the table, and the dead man lay stretched upon it, fully dressed. I remember noticing, the way one notices details in frightening moments, the flawless crease in his trousers and the shine on his black shoes. His arms were folded across his chest, his mouth was closed and he looked rather handsome and very young. At his head stood two tall brass candlesticks, their light putting the rest of the room in shadows. All the furniture had been removed except the kitchen chairs, which were lined up neatly along the far wall.

Madame Dey smiled at us slightly as we entered. With a shawl over her head, she looked like a great mourning widow.

We did not learn until the following day how it had come about. The hotel had not wanted to give her his clothes but she told them what the king said, that they could be sued for not taking the body in, and threatened to tell the young man's parents to do it unless they handed the clothing over to her. She had ironed his suit and polished his shoes before starting to dress him; only his shirt had presented a special problem. He had only the one he wore from the city and it was soiled, so she had to wash it and iron it dry, an exasperatingly slow job when there was so much to do.

As for the candlesticks, she had sent Amande to the curé to get them. "I told her to tell him that if he didn't lend me some, I'd go to the church to steal them," she reported. But the curé not only loaned them, he asked

64

his housekeeper to polish them first, and added the white candles on his own.

But, as I have said, we did not learn those details until the following day. That night we were too awed to ask, nor would we have had the time, for Madame Dey announced almost immediately: "I want to be at the station when the train arrives."

The platform was even more crowded than earlier, for by now the summer people all around the lake had heard the story. An avenue of space and silence opened around Madame Dey as she appeared.

When the great iron engine roared in, its wind and dust sweeping her skirts, and stopped, she stepped forward. The crowd watched and waited, quiet and motionless, as the conductor helped down a middle-aged woman with a handkerchief to her face, followed by a bewildered-looking man in city clothes.

Madame Dey walked toward them slowly, as one performing a ceremony. They looked up at her, their eyes helplessly questioning. She bowed slightly, and her voice seemed to come from an altar or a mountain as she said: "Votre fils est chez moi. Venez."

For the second time that night we watched her walk up the hill to her house. The three figures were sil-

houetted against the lights from the hotel and general store. Madame Dey walked behind the couple, as a mother follows an infant up a staircase, ready to give support should it fall back or stumble. They reached the open door, and in the light from inside, we saw the woman's head drop against her husband's shoulder and his arm go around her.

When Madame Dey entered, her massive size seemed to blot out all the light for a moment, and then the door was shut against the watching eyes.

That is where I would like to leave this account of Madame Dey, and yet I must, in faithfulness, go to the end. The next summer her house was gone and she was living alone in a two-room shack a mile south of the village. The daughter and son-in-law with whom she had shared the big house had moved thirty miles farther north. Amande was in Montreal working as a servant. My summers, too, were running out, and the year after that, my last at the lake, we found her torn by another tragedy.

During the winter, her son Gene had come home. He had arrived late in November ill with stomach cancer and died in April. He was twenty-seven.

The kindness she had shown strangers bereft of a son

only two years before was not in turn shown her. Alone and destitute, except for the food and wood sent her by her other sons in the village, she nursed him. "He went away a beautiful young boy, and he came back an old man to die in my arms," she told us, and yet her only bitterness was that "I did not still have my big house to look after him better."

Madame Dey moved away after that last summer to join her daughter and son-in-law farther north. Perhaps she had only stayed on after they left waiting for Gene to return; did she somehow know he would?

I never saw her again. But four or five years later, I returned to the village for a weekend and I stopped in to see one of her sons who was doing well as a carpenter now that so many ski chalets were being built. His mother was just fine, he told me. She was getting her old age pension, and she had used it to help set her son-in-law up in a small business. The city of Montreal had recently outlawed the hot dog and *patates frites* wagons that had been such a happy addition to its streets during my childhood. Some of the owners moved them outside the city limits; others sold them. With Madame Dey's help, her son-in-law had purchased one and ran it near a construction site in the village where they now lived.

"But what is she *doing?*" I asked.

"Oh, she helps out," her son told me. "She looks after the children, and she peels potatoes for the wagon."

She peels potatoes — the scene flashed before me like an old filmstrip from childhood. How often I had seen her peel things, potatoes for her family, apples for Amande and me. The peel would fall over her wrist in one continuous strip, so thin I would watch spellbound for it to break. It never did, until the apple was pared clean. When, finally, she presented it to me on her great brown hand, it no longer seemed like an apple at all; it was a sculpture of an apple, so lovingly had its nature been understood. And the peel would lie coiled on the newspaper at her feet, beautiful as newly woven ribbon.

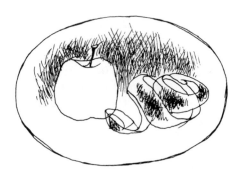

May Ebbitt Cutler was born in Montreal in 1923, the daughter of Irish immigrants. She holds master's degrees from McGill and Columbia universities, taught at McGill and wrote for several Canadian newspapers and magazines before opening the book publishing house, Tundra Books of Montreal, in 1967. A sister company, Tundra Books of Northern New York, was opened in 1971. Ms. Cutler is the wife of Superior Court Judge Philip Cutler, the mother of four sons, and continues to direct the operations of Tundra Books in both Canada and the U.S.

*Bruce Johnson is a well-known illustrator whose drawings have appeared in leading magazines in Canada (*Maclean's, Liberty, Chatelaine, Canadian Home Journal, Weekend*) — and in the United States* (Saturday Evening Post, Ladies Home Journal). *His sketches of Montreal scenes which appeared weekly in* The Montreal Star *for 15 years were published in book form in 1979 under the title* Montréal/Souvenirs *by Tundra Books. Mr. Johnson now lives in Colborne, Ontario where he continues to draw.*